KEY TO

HAPPINESS

Learn Simple Habits To Attain Happiness: In Personal, Professional Relationships, Minimize Stress, Gain Self–Discipline & Emotional Freedom.

JOSEPH NEYYAN

(neyyanjoseph@gmail.com)

Table of Contents

ACKNOWLEDGEMENT

First of all, I thank to the Almighty for making this book possible. I wish to thank my Mom, Mrs. Mary George and Dad Late Mr. NT George, who gave birth to me in this earth and made capable me to lead the journey of writing this book. My wife Mrs. Litty Joseph, who not only recognized in me that flair for writing my thoughts but also gave me the opportunity to write in my 'her time'. The support of my sons Mr. Prassil Joseph & Mr. Lijo Joseph and daughter-in-law Mrs. Mrinmayee Prassil made me to write this book.

The major personality whom I have met few months back excelled in the role of his mentorship, Mr. Som Bathla. His immense positivity and constant push made me structure the book and work further on my self-reliant publishing journey. I would not miss a chance to mention about Ref. Fr. George Mary Claret, Ms. Ayushi Ganguli, Mr. Vikram Khaitan, who have emerged out as a friend, philosopher and guide in this journey. Not to mention the endless support of Mr. Ranjit Jose, who designed the cover for this book with his relentless hardship available at all time basis and the courtesy by Photographer – CataFNqNEbDmYmE.

I don't want to miss out on all the friends who are pursuing Masters with me, mentioning about both the departments, even the one I wasn't physically a part of, yet all your encouragement on this news added new feathers on my cap. To my entire family and wonderful people who have imbibed positivity in me and those I couldn't take names of, I cannot thank you enough.

And lastly, to all the readers who chose to give my book a read and gather all the courage in analyzing the honest positive views.

Chapter 1: Introduction

Since the 1960, happiness research has been conducted in a wide variety of **scientific disciplines,** including gerontology, social psychology and positive psychology, clinical and medical research and happiness economics. 'Happiness is not something readymade. It comes from your own actions'. It is not how much we have, but how much we enjoy, that makes happiness. Joseph Neyyan, has created key evidence based actions that have been shown to increase happiness and wellbeing at home, at work, and relationships around you.

We all want to be happy but what does that mean and what can we do in our everyday lives to be happier? Fortunately, psychologist, neuroscientists and other experts now have evidence of what really makes a difference and help us to be happier and more **resilient** to life's up and downs.

Philosophy of happiness is often discussed in conjunction with ethics. Traditional European societies, inherited from the Greeks and from Christianity, often linked happiness with morality, which was concerned with the performance in a certain kind of role in a certain kind of social life. However, with the rise of individualism, begotten partly by Protestantism and capitalism, the links between duty in a society and happiness were gradually broken.

The consequence was a redefinition of the moral terms. Happiness is no longer defined in relation to social life, but in terms of individual psychology. Happiness, however, remains a difficult term for moral philosophy. Throughout the history of moral philosophy, there has been an oscillation between attempts to define morality in terms of consequences leading to happiness and attempts to define morality in terms that have nothing to do with happiness at all.

In this book, Joseph Neyyan has drawn on the latest scientific studies to create a set of evidence based on practical actions. They will help you connect with people, nature your relationships and find **solution**. You'll get ideas for taking care of your body, making the most of what's good, and finding alternative ways to **direct your mind**.

So here are the key to happier living-ideas, insights and practical actions that you can take to create more happiness for yourself and those around you.

An inspirational book that will **change your life**, the key to happiness contains an important message - it is time for you to wake-up and start living the life you right to live. Once you gain these important key, you will not only be astonishingly **happier** and **successful** in life. You also know that inner peace that **minimize stress, anxiety, fear, depression, frustrations, gain self-discipline & emotional freedom and confidence.**

Chapter -2: Happiness is the Prime Source for Living

"If you want to be happy for a minute, hear the music.

If you want to be happy for a day, go for a picnic.

If you want to be happy for a week, go for a tour.

If you want to be happy for a month, get married.

If you want to be happy for life long then love your profession" – Bill Gate

Many years ago, an enormous businessman lived in the United States. He had many factories of his own. The value of the property is in the billions. He was the richest man in the state. The age was past sixty. The rich man wanted to retire from his career one day. He and his wife settled down in a village several miles from the city, bought a piece of land by the river and built a huge bungalow of their choice. There he hired over eight servants to look after them and lived a life of royalty with no scope.

One morning, the rich man left his bungalow and was walking along a nearby pond, enjoying nature. Then he saw a boat tied in the shadow of a tree. A young man was sleeping inside the boat. When he saw him, he realized that he was a fisherman, and that this was his boat. He sleeps lazily in the morning without working hard and progressing during this age of energy in the body. The rich man wondered how big of a fool he would be.

He knocks him up and asked, 'you seem to be a young man who is physically strong. Why are you sleeping like this in the morning? To the rich man he replied, Sir, it is my duty to fish at midnight. I would catch fish all night and come ashore in the morning and sleep in the shade for a while. And then I sell the fish at the market and I would take the money and go home. Again, the rich man asked, how would you spend your day? For that he said he would sleep well when he reached home, spend time with family, and if there were any fun events happening in this town: he would see them.

The rich man asked again, why are you wasting your youth like this? If he could go fishing during the day instead? Hearing this, the young man said that the money I earn every day is enough for my family!

On top of this, he innocently asked why I should earn? The rich man replied, 'If you earn more than what you need, you can keep savings left over and buy a new motor, go deeper into the pond and catch more fish. Then you will have more money. Keep it up and buy a quality net and catch more fish. Then you can buy many more modern boats, hire people and fish all over the pond. After that you too will become a huge business tycoon like me, eventually buying a house by the river and ending up saying you can spend the rest of your life here in peace.

The man who was patiently listening to all this! What did you think I'm doing now? This question threw the rich man away. His past life appeared before his eyes. He spent most of his youth making money. Not spending time with family. He was never around when the kids were growing up. He had earned billions in these sixty years. He had seen many countries in the world.

What gave us peace of mind today is the life that lives on the banks of this river. This fisherman is living the same life. The enlightenment that came to me after seeing so many struggles of life past 60 years is what this fisherman has at such a young age. So, who is superb at his? As he asked himself the question, he walked towards his house with a smile on his face.

This life is a beautiful journey. Everyone lives according to their needs. If one lives this for the needs of the next, he cannot live this life with satisfaction. No matter how big a dream you have in life, no matter how many billions you want to earn in it, make sure that your dreams and hard work do not ruin the life you are living. Do not forget one thing, without enjoying the auspicious moments of life, running towards his goal like a racing horse will surely end up as a disappointment.

Chapter -3: Unhappy Person Always Remember These 4 Things

"The art of being happy lies in the power of extracting happiness from common things" - Henry Wood Beecher

In this World, every person gets sorrow and pain, no person can escape from this law of nature. Just think what would be sad if God only gives happiness? How to know so the joy of life is present in both sorrow and happiness, because sorrow only teaches you to fight this world. Bad times are the times when humans test their inner skills when you are going through hard times, then remember these four information carefully and respect it too.

Unhappy person remembers these four things

1. Nothing in this world is stable, everything changes every second, so instead of being afraid of such times, enjoy time while being patient and try to test the surrounding people.

2. When you have, everyone likes you, but very few people will get to know the real identity of many artificial faces, there will be some great personalities who will see you and change your path.

3. When a man is having a good time, he thinks he will lack nothing, but when the time comes bad, then he leaves even the clothes of the body and this is the universal truth of life which every person should accept.

4. Bad time comes for everyone, so instead of being afraid, learn to face it, you may have been far behind, but good to be sad and try to stand once again.

Chapter -4: How to Be Happy When Everything Goes Wrong

"The talent for being happy is appreciating and liking what you have, instead of what you don't have" – *Woody Allen.*

Imagine your house being destroyed in an earthquake or wounded in a car crash and losing your legs. Many people will characterize the effect of such an event. Some people say they'd prefer to be dead instead of never living again.

It is important to remember that in the years a study was discovered, it was not repeated, but they followed the general pattern over and over. We continue to overestimate the effect or traumatic events on our lives. This is significant. Very optimistic and highly negative incidents to not affect our long-term satisfaction as much as we think.

If You Want To Happy Then Need To Do These Things

Investigators term this 'The Effect Bias' as we appear to overestimate the duration or strength of satisfaction triggered by key events. The impact bias is an example of emotional prediction, a social psychological phenomenon that refers to our ability to forecast potential emotional situations as human beings.

We imagine the event and all the money that will be given when we think about winning the lottery. But we forget the other 99% of our lives and how it will remain the same. When we don't get enough sleep, we can always feel grumpy. During rush hour traffic, we still have to wait. Whether we want to stay in shape, we still need to work out. Each year we will still give our taxes. When we lose a loved one, it will always hurt. On the porch it'll always be cool to relax and watch the sunset. But we fought things that stay the same, we imagine the transition.

Second, an obstacle to something, not to you as a person, is a challenge. 'Going lame is not your will' says the Greek philosopher Epictetus. We overestimate exactly why negative events affect our lives because we overestimate the amount of positive events that would be of benefit to our lives. We focus on what happens (like the loss of a leg), but forget all those life experiences.

Both these are pleasant stuff that can be done with or without a leg. Mobility concerns only reflect an infinitesimal fraction of the interactions. Nasty incidents can pose difficulties for specific tasks, but the experience of the human individual is large and diverse. A life that appears rather alien or unwelcome to your present imagination is plenty of room for happiness.

Chapter -5: Five Secret of Happiness

"The only thing that will make you happy is being happy with who you are, and not who people think you are"- Goldie Hawn.

There is no one in this world who is not facing any problem. Problem is everywhere, but it's up to us how do we deal with it. We should always face many problems with problem-solving strategies or smartly. We face many up and downs in life, which left us in a state of anxiety and stress.

<u>We all have the power of healing</u>. Something we use this power unknowingly, and sometimes we use it if we are aware of it. Here is the effective solution of your every negative thoughts and anxiety. Whenever you are in bad or unfavorable situation, use this solution, you would feel better.

<u>Go for a walk</u>. When we spend time alone, then we always understand ourselves much better because before solving any problem it's important to know yourself. If you go for a walk, your mind and soul feel all the positive things. It gives you a chance to meditate over various things while spending time with yourself. Our thoughts and emotions are attached biologically, and that's why it has power to develop self-healing. So, always try to go for a walk in the morning or evening.

<u>Talk with positive people.</u> When you have a conversation with positive people, then you automatically feel positive and motivated. Your negative thoughts, depression can be solved easily. If you have surrounded yourself with positive people, then they can also give you some advice or can solve your problems.

<u>Listen to yourself and try to help people</u>. When you help others, then you feel satisfied. It gives you inner satisfaction. When you are internally satisfied then you can easily listen to your inner voice and it becomes easy to communicate yourself.

Healthy diet and maintain balance in life. We are what we eat. If we not healthy then we couldn't focus on our work or can't maintain a healthy relationship with anyone. So it's important to take care of our health. A healthy person can maintain personal and professional life in a much better way than any unhealthy people. Therefore, it's important to give some time to yourself, family, friends and your professional life.

Plans and discipline. Every successful person believes in a power of discipline. Make your plans according to your goals, be focused and hard work is needed.

So, if you want to enjoy your life and want to be the happiest person, then use these steps and always stay happy and live a successful life.

Chapter -6: Two Things Makes Human Happier

"Happiness cannot be traveled to, owned, earned, worn or consumed. Happiness is the spiritual experience of living every minute with love, grace, and gratitude" – Denis Waitley.

A great person always does two things, first forgiving mistakes and secondly forgetting those mistakes. When the world tilts completely, only then is the right time to pray. So we have happiness by being patient and always avoid speaking more because speaking too much can lead to mistakes. One thing to remember is to always have something to say while a stupid person will never feel the need to say whatever things you want to others. It's not like to learn to dislike them in themselves as it is necessary to eat for the nutrition of the body. Similarly, helping others will be beneficial for the nutrition of the soul.

Quite often, keeping yourself silent is the most powerful answer. Just take care of your tongue in the same way that you take care of gold and silver. Always keep in mind one thing, the price is not thirst for water, there is no meaning in life. But death is everything, it is never a matter of relationship, but of faith, whoever boost of others is never able to relax and no one loves who does not have manners.

If you do not have anything, then it does not matter, at least it will be much better than begging others. Our enemy is not from any religion but our biggest enemy is ignorance. Telling the truth brings goodness and good thinking person. Heaven is destined for all your expectations should be from God only and there is no need to be afraid of anything in the world except your sin. Whenever you are sick, there is no need to fear or panic. Try to expect more and more.

When there is no emotion in the heart, the tears dry up, while the heart becomes a stone by repeated sins. The poor person lives in his own country like a foreigner, there is no need to be so strict that someone will break you and so fragile, don't have to be someone to press you.

Chapter -7: Get Rid Of Depression Know Therapy

Depression is classified as a mood disorder. It may be described as feelings of sadness, loss, or anger that interfere with a person's everyday activities. It's also fairly common. The Centers for Disease Control and Prevention (CDC) estimates that 8.1 percent of American adults ages 20 and over had depression in any given 2 week period from 2013 to 2016.

Depression was said to cause many serious events up to attempt to suicide. There has been a kind of fear among people about depression. People cannot get out of the houses during this stage. Refer to one of the government employee become Model, and Bollywood actor Mr. Dinesh Mohan at the age was 60 years went on depression for 8 months in his room alone and not willing to come outside of the room due to his family expired. He becomes 130 kg over weight. He was lying on the bed and could not even walk in his room during these months. His sister and brother-in-law helped him to cure him to reduce his weight by 60 kg through a trainer to train him physical exercises and the nutrition diet.

So the question arises in the peoples' mind that if someone goes into depression, is it difficult to overcome it? Is this disease curable? So the answer is yes. When someone is surrounded by depression, he feels that he will never come out of that situation. However, treatment can be up to severe depression. So if depression is spoiling the beauty of life, then seek the help of a doctor. There are many treatment options in depression, from meditations to healthy lifestyle changes. Just as now depression affects two people, there cannot be a similar treatment to cure them. One treatment may prove beneficial for a person, but it may be on the other. There are many treatments that can help overcome depression, make you feel happy and hopeful, and help you regain your life. Depression can be usually treated with meditations, but there are other ways to recover from it. The steps are given below:-

1. **<u>Therapy</u>**. If meditations are to be avoided for symptoms of depression, therapy can be a highly effective treatment. Therapy helps to feel better and prevent depression. Many types of therapy are available for dynamic Therapy doctors. Such as Cognitive-Behavioral Therapy, Interpersonal Therapy and Psychodynamic Therapy. Often all three are treated together. Some types of therapy teach practical techniques to overcome negative thinking and combat depression.

2. **<u>Not just medicines</u>**. Depression is not just about a chemical imbalance in the brain. The drug may help relieve some symptoms of moderate and severe depression, but does not cure the problem. There are also side effects of antidepressants, but even if it is necessary to take them, we cannot ignore other treatments. Lifestyle changes and therapy will not only provide quick relief from depression, but will also help in preventing the possibility of recurrence. Lifestyle changes: we must include

exercise in the lifestyle. Exercise not only promotes serotonin, endorphins and feel-good brain chemicals but also increases connections between new brain cells and them, just like antidepressants.

3. **<u>Interaction with friends</u>**: It is common in depression that the victim is cut off from the society, but to get out of this darkness, keep in regular contact with friends and family or consider joining a group. Here family and friends have an important role to give positive atmosphere to the victim. The biggest thing is to make him realize how special he is to him, and he has no problem in accepting the way he is. A balance diet is very important for physical and mental health, and it can help in maintaining energy and improving mood.

4. **<u>Sleep well</u>**. Try to get a good sleep every night 7-8 hours of sleep is necessary. Make such changes in daily routine, which reduces stress. Do not stay amid work or relationships that stress.

5. It's difficult to get out of depression but not impossible, so give yourself time to get out of this and don't give up hope to get out of this darkness.

Chapter -8: How to Deal with Depression with 5 Easy Steps

Depression is a common illness worldwide, with more than 264 million people affected. Depression is different from usual mood fluctuations and short-lived emotional responses to challenges in everyday life. Especially when long-lasting and with moderate or severe intensity, depression may become a serious health condition. It can cause the affected person to suffer greatly and function poorly at work, at school and in the family. At its worst, depression can lead to suicide. Close to 800,000 people die due to suicide every year. Suicide is the second leading cause of death in 15 to 29 year olds.

There are so many ways that we can help ourselves. There are tons of ways, but these are just some helpful tips to get you started.

<u>Keeping busy all day</u>. I know that sounds really simple, but often our anxiety loves and lives in the quiet. When we have nothing to do, and we are sitting at home, and we are moping about, it kind of takes a molehill, and turns it into a mountain. When we have time to ruminate and think about things, it can make it so much worse. But if we are just going about our day, we're breaking hearts. We don't have time to think about it. So I would encourage you, if you are able, plan your days out, make sure you have things happening back to back. You're scooting on through.

What we call 'feeling', and this is something that we can do no matter where we are. Which I love about tips, because we never know when the anxiety may strike. The feeling focus is when we focus on the area in our body where we feel the anxiety. For some of us it might be our throat, chest, stomach. It could be on our shoulders wherever you feel it physically. And I know this is just one of those things where you are like, 'Kati that sounds weird'. I promised you by drawing your focus back to the area in your body. Your anxiety will diminish. It's because our mind can't go out searching for more things to worry us with. It will dissipate slowly.

Exercise. Now obviously I don't want you to do anything to an extreme, but taking a thirty-minute walk. If you like to run and it's not unhealthy, you go for a run. Maybe you jump some rope, maybe you take your dog out, maybe you walk with a friend, maybe you do yoga, whatever it is. If you play tennis, play basketball, there's so many things to do. Anything you can do to exert some physical energy, which can help with anxiety. Often timing an outlet for that, even if it's just nervous energy. Haves when we have a lot of pent up energy, anxiety thrives. So having an outlet like exercise can really help bring it down.

Phoning a friend. I feel like we are on who wants to be Millionaire? But it's important to contact people and to have people on what I always talk to my clients about, on your 'emergency call list'. And this isn't a real, this isn't like an emergency 'I'm going to the hospital I'm bleeding. I broke a bone'. This is 'I'm feeling stressed, I'm feeling overwhelmed, I don't know what to do right now'.

We need to have at least five people on this list if you can. Because we never know who can pick up, right? Some people might be in class. Some people might be asleep. Some people might be at work. We don't know, but we want to make sure we have people that we can contact. Even if it's a text, I know that we text more than we call. But I want you to reach out to people. Because having someone on the line. Having someone talking to us. I think calling is the best. Because hearing someone's voice can be so soothing. And sometimes when we feel like we are a ton on our anxiety scale. It can help bring us back down to maybe a six or a five. And the more we talk with them about what's going on with us. The better we will felt.

Consult a Psychiatrist. The reason that I wanted to put this in here is because there are most of us who doing these things, feeling, focusing, we're exercising, we're trying everything to help ourselves. We're seeing our own therapist, and nothing gives. It's not getting better, and sometimes it's getting worse. And consulting a psychiatrist, they can offer medications that can help with it.

The medication can help us get there. All research shows that therapy and medication give us the best outcome. Because sometimes our mind is running so quickly. Things are happening so fast. That we can't even think about doing anything to help ourselves. We're just trying to stay afloat. It's so overwhelming, and medication can help with that. Bring the anxiety level down enough so we can take action. We can start making steps towards our recovery, putting things in place, creating plans. It can give us that little of squish we need to get started. So I would encourage you if you have tried a lot of things.

Depression in Pregnant Women Can Lead To Aggressive Son

Depression in pregnancy can be dangerous. The sons' of women who have depression during pregnancy are highly active. This has been claimed in a recent research. Researchers in Canada also found that children up to the age of 18 were more likely to develop depression than their mothers who suffered from prenatal depression.

The team of researchers said that about 20 percent of women suffer from depression during pregnancy and the effects on their fetus are still unclear. According to prior research, depression caused to the mother during pregnancy causes behavioral and development problems in children.

Son's brain network is weak. According to researchers, depressed mothers' sons' have weak brain connections that affect their behavior. The study found that weak white matter in children's brains was also associated with increased aggression and hyperactivity.

The Canadian University of Kalgeri team studies 54 pregnant women and their children. During pregnancy, it surveyed women several times in which asked them about their symptoms of depression. After the birth of the children, the researchers performed their diffuse MRI, which gave information about their brain network.

Cannot control emotions. Researchers said depression in prenatal mothers was found to be associated with lower white matter in sons' brains. White matter processes emotional processes in the brain. In such a situation, because of weak white matter, children cannot control emotions. These weaknesses can cause so called `distorted emotional states' in children in which they become unable to manage the intensity and duration of negative emotions such as fear, sadness or anger. This explains why children of depressed mothers have a higher risk of developing diseases.

Better care needed. Researchers said that the findings of this research suggest that depression in prenatal mothers should be identified and treated so it does not affect their son's development. Researchers said, 'Changes in the brain structure of children because of depression of mothers affect their behavior'. Prenatal mothers should be better taken care of.

Chapter -9: How to Build Confidence and Self Confidence

"Happiness is not something you postpone for the future; it is something you design for the present"- Jim Rohn.

The haunting hesitation, the inferiority of the talent, but the inexplicable horror. Even when we have experienced such things, we tend to, but we're not looking for, outside. How much information? It is about gaining confidence and what the gainers look like. Definition of one's own. Some people are confident that speaking up is courageous, while living confidently is confidence on another's part. What confidence do we all hear in the outside world?

There is confidence in the soul: it does not gain confidence from the outside. The original has confidence in the soul. He who loses everything will live for one tomorrow. When we are feeling very humiliated or sad, we are sitting there worrying that everything is over. Isn't that confidence within our soul? But as we grow, it embeds our confidence in our layers as we fill in what we don't need. It devotes something to saving the hope of surviving into a tough situation. Exterior-Inside Impurities: If you feel like that, you must knock on the door of our house and say you're incapable and unsafe.

The negative words that are heard when we are in a bit of a weak mood can leave a great deal of anxiety in the mind. We never leave the words there. We become helpless by repeatedly listening to the recorder in our head. This outer scum goes into the inside of us. This negative impurity becomes a part of us, and we question ourselves about what we will do. Do I have confidence? Once this happened. The disciple asks at the Guru.

There is a big hill near my house. I have a desire to climb it, but not yet. Whenever I wanted to climb, I would go to the bottom of the hill and look up and ask: 'Can I climb this hill? Ten confident?' My mind would say, 'Is the hill climbing? What if a foot slips? What if it's dead?

Half way back? No excitement of pre-climbing. What's the point? Whenever I do, I will give up my idea of climbing and leave. When are my gurus saying words that make my mind confident? Can I really climb? Is called a guru: 'What? Did I ever question whether I was confident before climbing a hill? Who trusted to climb the said hill.

One step up the stairs is enough. Reach the top of the hill and leave. You ask your opinion and ask if I can climb! Why do you feel the mind? Just watch the climb. Look at the cotton. The question is unnecessary; this our problem. Leaving life unnecessary questioned. Doubts about whether there are trustworthiness. Trust in us! The fears and anxieties are in question. There is a tendency to abandon what you think is right! We will not continue until we work to glorify fears. As the pupil lifted his way down the hill to question.

Confidence in one: we need not experience infinite power before doing any war. Our sense of confidence as a job is done in a short time.

Fear and apprehension are common when leaving to do additional work. If one continues without standing there, the fears will go away. What everything for the first time can cause a lot of apprehension, but it is not possible to do the same thing repeatedly. Such new things scare us first, and then not cool! Whatever it is, we need to take a step forward by consolidating the power we have. Fear has to go through itself and move on. If we put one hand, our confidence is in our hands. The infinite confidence that lies in our soul.

How to Build The Self-Confidence You Need

Everyone builds billions of dollars, becomes YouTube stars, or makes it big on. Big on Instagram. But all those people live wonderful lives, and it's right or not.

If you want to win at life, self-esteem is vital no matter what you are seeking, it will always hold you back by a lack of confidence. Research shows even that there is a lack of confidence:

- Anxiety

- Solitude and a feeling of loss
- Lower college quality
- Satisfaction of lower life

I have been looking for self-confidence for years and the theory I found most practical is that called 'confidence by skill'

Self-confidence building. So, if you get better with what you do, you get more confident. This is the method, and work supports it. The method below is easy, but the steps are difficult to complete.

- Enhance your expertise
- Contribute to them
- See result
- More trustworthy
- Return.

If you would like to apologize, it's okay. This is your life. This is your future. But this self-confidence building method is based on real and tangible steps and not on immaterial things like assertions. Trust does not magically emerge on its own.

Every day, you can say to yourself that you are confident, but you never really will believe yourself if you lack the skills to get worse.

This is my fundamental concern with other myths and authors in self-help. Affirmations, co-instructive thinking and setting goals are all fine, but they're not executive.

Emotional intelligence. Study shows that people are social. We are dying without good relations. So you need emotional intelligence if you want healthy relationships: to recognize so react to emotional feelings of others. You should understand this is everything.

Self-consciousness. By continuous self-reflections you can practice self-consciousness. Write your thinking: try to understand why you do, what you do and what you can do differently.

Problem solving. Our current network of school dates back to the industrial revolution.

They have educated us in a wheel to be cogs. In complex situations, it does not train us to solve problems, rather; we do what we are told. However, the world has shifted, and the person who solves the problem better will win in the current state. Don't fool yourself into thinking as long as you want, your life will be better.

You believe in your ability to get things done when you work and see the results—like an increased body, more strength, more money, more happiness or whatever.

Chapter -10: Five Things Do in the Morning for a Headstart

"There is only one happiness in this life, to love and be loved" – *George Sand.*

What are the things one should do in the morning immediately after waking up, so he/she can live the whole day with full energy and enthusiasm? What are the things one can do to eliminate procrastination which you feel immediately after waking up? How can one get rid of the urge to sleep back again? Here are some solutions to these problems.

Plan Ahead. Immediately after waking up plan what you want to do later in the day. Either enthusiasm of doing that thing or tension of completing the task will not let you sleep again. It is very effective of getting rid of laziness. It also helps in creating a clear picture of your goals as it focuses you on a particular thing only that is planning.

<u>Drink Water Straight Away</u>. Our body gets dehydrated overnight, which is one of causes of laziness. So make sure as soon as you wake up drink water to hydrate your body. As a step higher, mix lemon, ice or cucumber in it for better effects.

<u>Get off the Bed</u>. Until and unless you can get off the bed, you cannot win the race against the urge of sleeping back again. So remember, get off the bed as soon as you wake up. Do not give a chance to your brain to think about sleeping again. And when that thought comes, surprise, you are already standing.

<u>Motivate Yourself</u>: Besides setting goals, motivate yourself but speaking to you. You can do this while brushing, bathing, etc. It is beneficial for waking your mind. If paste a poster of your goal or a motivating quote on the wall of your room and make sure it is the first thing you see in the morning. It will have benefits you will enjoy in the long run.

<u>Eat Breakfast</u>: Maybe the most important of all. You require energy to do things. Where to get this energy from, simple by eating breakfast. Eating breakfast provides you with invaluable energy our body requires which throughout the day to perform tasks.

To conclude, mourning time is the most important time for you to decide regarding what you do and what you miss out by sleeping more. So take these decisions wisely for every day happiness.

Chapter -11: A Guide on How to Sleep Better Every Night

"Happiness is a choice. You can choose to be happy. There's going to be stress in life, but it's your choice whether you let it affect you or not" – Valerie Bertinelli.

One of the oddest things we do every day is sleep. The average adult will spend 36% of his life. We have switched from the vibrant, reflective and active creatures, we are in the summer to a peaceful state of winter resting for one-third of our time on Earth.

Sleep has many important functions for your brain and body. Let's take some big one down. Sleep is restored as the first reason. Your brain accumulates metabolic waste every day, as it performs normal neural activity. Although it is normal, there has been too much waste accumulation in connection with neurological disturbances like Alzheimer's disease.

The body relaxes during slow wave sleep; the breathing becomes frequent, and the brain decreases blood pressure, making it more difficult to wake up. The regeneration and repair of the body is essential in this process. The hypophysis releases a growth hormone during slow wave sleep which stimulates tissue growth and muscle repair. Researchers also conclude that by this point the body's immune system has been restored. If you are an athlete, slow wave sleep is especially important. We often hear professional athletes such as Roger Federer or LeBron James to sleep 11 or 12 hours a night.

For the mind, REM sleep is slow for the body. During most sleep periods, the brain is relatively calm, but your brain comes alive during REM. REM sleep is when the brain dreams of knowledge and re-organizes it. During this stage your brain eliminates any irrelevant information, improves your memory by comparing the last 24 hours of experiences with previous experiences and encourages neural developed and learning. The body will increase temperatures, blood pressure and heart rates will trice. Your body barely moves through all this movement. The REM phase usually happens about 3 to 5 times a night in brief explosions.

During sleep, the brain cells gradually decrease 60 percent, making it much easier for the brain to 'take out the garbage.' This is called the lymph mechanism. In your sleep, your brain is refreshed, and you wake up with a logical mind.

Muscle, inadequate sleep or sleeveless cycles can increase the risk of diabetes and heart disease and lead to insulin insensitivity and metabolic syndrome.

The researchers began the experiment with 48 healthy men and women who averaged 7 to 8 sleep hours per night. Then, the subjects are divided into four different groups. The first party had to stay sleepless for 3 days. For 4 hours a night, the second group slept. Sleeping 6 hours per night was the third group. Eight hours a night, the fourth group had to sleep. Such sleep patterns were holding for two consecutive weeks in the last three groups-4, 6 and 8 hours of sleep.

We have tested the participants for physical and mental competence in the experiment.

A study performed on the Stanford basketball players considers the effect of sleep on physical performance. The players slept at least ten hours' per night during this study (compared to their typical 8 hours). The investigators measured the accuracy and pace of basketball players during five weeks of extended sleep in relation to their previous rates. The shooting percentage of three points increased 9.2%. And when sprinting 80 meters, the players were 0.6 seconds quicker. Slow wave sleep helps you recover when your place heavy physical demands on your body. Your brain will be happy the whole day by following these rule.

Chapter -12: Thoughts Would Like the Most

"Happiness radiates like the fragrance from a flower and draws all good things towards you" – Maharishi Mahesh Yogi.

Everyone is having many thought ideas. Many of us are there whose day starts with beautiful thoughts. May it be about some inspirational, motivational or love thoughts. Thoughts give us the inspiration to learn. It makes our day feel with much more love and happiness. There are some thoughts which I like the most.

Nothing is impossible, everything is possible. That's true, nothing in this world is impossible, everything is possible. Just we have to do is try to try harder and have patience in ourselves to make that thing possible. As the word itself only says that, `I'm possible.

Failure is the best teacher than success. Failure teaches us many things in life.

It gives us the motivation and the power to make try to things successful. It is the only path to success. It teaches us that the mistake which we had done in our life earlier won't be repeated further, and we can do the best from that mistake.

<u>Don't compare life with others</u>. We shouldn't try to compare our life with others. Everyone is born with their own talents. Like all the five fingers are not the same. In the same way everyone in this world is not same. Everyone has their own talent, their own passion.

<u>Age is not a factor for which we should get tensed</u>. We are most eligible to achieve something new at any age. The person who is considering age as a factor to learn something new couldn't be able to achieve the success human being wants.

<u>Should do the things you like the most</u>. Fulfilling others dreams may lead you to success, but it won't give you the actual happiness or the success you want in life. So get busy with the things you love which give you the intense happiness and creates an interest within you to work with that.

<u>Love yourself first</u>. No one in this world is there to stay with you for the entire life. Parents are there to support you, but they will not stand by your side every time you want. You yourself have to stand by your side. Never get upset with your beauty or the complexion you have. Everyone is beautiful in their own way. So love yourself with what you are and the things you have! So, get inspired with this most beautiful thoughts and happy in the life.

Chapter -13: How to Take Care of Your Brain

"Thousands of candles can be lighted from a single candle, and the life of the candle will not be shortened. Happiness never decreases by being shared" – Buddha.

The following thing you need to take great consideration of your brain. We live in the information society and dealing with your brain is critical. Your psyche is the best resource for make, convey and catch however much incentive as expected on the business sectors; and you ought to likewise deal with your brain to settle on brilliant life choices.

- To turn into the best form of yourself, there are two viewpoints to taking appropriate consideration of your brain. The following is the principle:
- Ensure you control your brain and that your psyche doesn't control you.

- Limit psychological mutilations with enthusiastic bookkeeping.
- Normally update your mind's 'product' or reinvent your negative behavior patterns.
- Conceptualize thoughts regularly.
- Continuously attempt new things throughout everyday life.

On the off chance that you need to accomplish your pinnacle potential, you need to assume responsibility for your psyche; your brain will thwart your potential as opposed to supporting you in accomplishing your pinnacle execution.

On the off chance that you don't assume control over the control of your psyche, the brain will rather concentrate on negative reasoning, psychological contortions and mental masturbation (diversion).

The most ideal approach of assume responsibility for your psyche is to rehearse contemplation, center on appreciation and what you as of now have throughout everyday life, build up the wealth outlook, become mindful of your predominant intellectual bends and dispense with them with enthusiastic bookkeeping, and take standard updates of your cerebrum's 'product'.

Truly, regardless of whether the cerebrum is an incredible organ, the product is runs among neurons is very cart. By perusing, turning in two addresses, conversing with individuals, watching various circumstances, reflecting and other comparable circumstances, you can refresh your product to be less carriage.

You additionally need to normally improve your imaginative potential. We would all be able to be innovative; you need to rehearse. There are two simple methods of building up your inventive potential, without turning into a craftsman or something. Record new thoughts consistently and continually attempt new things throughout everyday life.

To summarize, here are some entirely significant things you can do to build up your psyche to the most extreme and become the best form of yourself in this viewpoint.

Ruminate—Take out psychological twists individually with passionate bookkeeping.

- Record one thing you are thankful

for consistently.

Be a deep rooted student—continually build up your skills, read and read a great deal, go to talks and workshops, take online courses, regard information and ensure you get a ton.

Breaking point mental masturbation exercises like sitting in front of the TV, watching the day by day news, investing energy in informal organizations, taking part in futile gatherings and so on. Ensure you become the ace of the time the executives.

Consistently record at any rate 30 thoughts. Open a note pad and concept continuously attempt new things throughout everyday life—take another course home, attempt another game or a leisure activity, brush your teeth with your non-predominant hand, do something contrary to what you typically do, travel, become familiar with another dialect,

play mind-advancement games and so forth.
There are such huge numbers of things you can
do and attempt.

Chapter -14: Tips to Live a Stress Free Life

*"**Happiness doesn't depend on any external conditions, it is governed by our mental attitude**" – Dale Carnegie.*

Despite the fact that stress has adverse effects on our life, we still deny admitting that this could be a mental disorder. Leading a stressful life hinders our efficiency and lessens our ability to live a healthy and happy life. Being stressed, you may fall sick more often, can feel grumpy and even irritated too.

In today's lifestyle, stress is an integral part of our life. Tension sometimes becomes so much that it starts bothering you. That is why it is believed that mental stress hurts you more than a limit, but in today's life, stress has become so ingrained that the symptoms of stress appear everywhere. Often, in a loud voice, annoyance, restlessness, angry anger, all these things are symptoms of stress today.

1. **<u>Routine</u>**. We all should make a pursuit every day. A hobbies present a structured and geared up way of living. We can make use of our day fruitfully. We should hold a time table for leisure in our routine. It will assist us to live a stress-free life. We can whole all our work on time and can indulge in some leisure activities.

2. **<u>Wake up early</u>**. We can wake up early to entirely all our work on time. Waking up early is now not healthful for your physique, however is additionally recommended in enhancing intellectual health. As the saying goes. "early to bed and early to rise, makes a man, healthy, wealthy and wise".

3. **<u>Face the challenges</u>**. If you discover yourself in the worst state of affairs or if some of your choices have lent you in trouble, receive and discover the answer for it rather of cribbing. It will enhance our confidence. We will be meditate enthusiastic about our work. Make a list of things that make you happy and optimistic.

4. **<u>Meditation.</u>** We can meditate ourselves every day for 1 hour. It will make us calm and concentrated. When you are targeted on your work, you can accomplish greater and in an environment friendly manner. Concentrate on the work that you function and supply it to your best. This helps to end your venture quicker and in an environment friendly manner. Besides this, it also helps to reduce your anxiety, tension and stress.

5. **<u>Relaxation</u>**. Relaxation is an indispensable phase of our routine. We have to loosen up our thinking and body. We can make us cozy be means of doing yoga nature. We can relax for 1-2 hours in a day. We ought to sleep for at least 6 hours in a day. We ignore our own selves either by eating unhealthy meals or by not giving our body and mind enough rest.

6. **<u>Distraction</u>**. All distractions must be stored away from our life. These distractions are in the structure of cell phones, laptops, and television. When we cannot make a stability between the digital and bodily world, it becomes a little hard

to absolutely get rid of these distractions from our life.

7. **<u>Stop living in the past and Future</u>**. We have to stay in the existing moment. It will assist us to take delivery of the truth of life. Being in the previous or the future entails dwelling in your head and ignoring what's going on in your physique and emotions.

8. **<u>Unnecessary jealousy will boost stress</u>**. Some people are always jealous of other people or people's actions or their success or happiness and are looking for such opportunities how to let them down or hinder their work. It is not good to have this type of competition. In such a situation we will always be under anxiety and stress, which will not be good for your body at all. Therefore keep positive thinking, so that the mind gets energy and the whole body stays in the energy and happiness.

How to Overcome Obstacles and Frustrations

Sometimes in life we discover ourselves faced with obstacles or situations don't accept as true with but cannot do much about. It is often a choice somebody else has made that affects you in how or an unfavorable circumstance. If you're feeling stuck or frustrated during a situation like this and it looks like your world is falling apart remember no matter what's happening you've got control over how you select to react and thus, how quickly you pull yourself out of negative feelings. Below are the steps I exploit to tug myself up and stay and happy whatever obstacle comes my way.

First things first, if you're feeling sad or frustrated, the worst thing you'll do is to suppress the strong emotions you're feeling. We sleep in a society that teaches us that crying or emotionally may be a sign of weakness and vulnerability, the danger this poses is that if you don't let the emotions out, they accumulate inside you and with time can cause a significant breakdown or maybe physical illnesses. So if you would like to cry, just cry the maximum amount as you would like. Let it all out, you'll be amazed how relieved you are feeling afterwards.

When someone frustrates you, always take a breath first before you react. Decide if you want to talk now or wait to calm down. If you're highly reactive and upset, have the discussion later when you're calmer. Then you'll be more persuasive and less threatening. At that time use this approach, which is from emotional freedom.

What Is The Fastest Way To Relieve Stress?

Figure out how to use the intensity of your faculties to ease weight on the sport and remain quiet, gainful, and concentrated–regardless of what life tosses at you.

What is the quickest method to relieve stress?

There are innumerable strategies for overseeing pressure. Yoga, care, contemplation, and exercise are only two pressure soothing exercises that do some incredible things. Without giving it much thought, during a high-forced prospective employee meet up, for instance, or a conflict with your mate, you can't pardon yourself to reflect or go for a long stroll. In these circumstances, you need something more quick and available.

One of the speediest and most solid approaches to get rid of pressure is to draw in at least one of your faculties–sight, sound, taste, smell, contact–or through development. Since everybody is extraordinary, you must do some testing to find which strategy works best for you– however the result is gigantic. Your van remains quiet, gainful, and centered when you realize how to rapidly alleviate pressure.

Social connection is your body's most developed and surefire procedure for controlling the sensory system. Talking up close and personal with a loose and caring audience can help you rapidly quiet down and delivery pressure. Although you can't have a buddy to incline toward in a distressing circumstance, keeping up a system of cozy connections is imperative for your psychological wellbeing. Between tangible based pressure help and great audience members, you'll have your bases secured.

Tip 1: Perceive when you're pushed

It may appear glaringly clear that you'd realize when you're pushed, yet a considerable lot of us invest such a great amount of energy in a fatigued express that we've overlooked what it feels like when our sensory systems are in balance: when we're quiet yet still ready and centered. If this is you, you can perceive when you're worried by tuning in to your body. At the point when you're drained, your eyes feel overwhelming and you may lay your head on your hand. At the point when you're cheerful, you giggle with no problem. Also, when you're focused on your body tells you that. Start focusing on your body's pieces of information.

<u>Watch your muscles and internal parts</u>. Are your muscles tense or sore? Is your stomach tight, squeezed, or hurting? Are your hands or jaw gripped?

<u>Watch your breath</u>. Is your breathing shallow? Spot one hand on your gut, the other on your chest. Watch your hands rise and fall with every breath. Notice when you inhale completely or when "it slips your mind" to relax.

Tip 2: Distinguish your pressure reaction

Inside, we as a whole react a similar path to the "battle or-flight" stress reaction: your circulatory strain rises, your heart siphons quicker, and your muscles choke. Your body tries sincerely and channels your resistant framework. Remotely individuals react to worry in various ways.

The most ideal approach to rapidly mitigate pressure regularly identifies with your particular pressure reaction.

<u>Overexcited pressure reaction</u>. If you will become furious, fomented, excessively enthusiastic, or keyed up under pressure, you will react best to pressure alleviation exercises that calm you down.

<u>Under excited stress reaction</u>. If you will become discouraged, pulled back, or scattered under pressure, you will react best to pressure help exercises that are invigorating and stimulating.

Tip 3: Carry your faculties to the salvage

To use your faculties to rapidly calm pressure, you first need to distinguish the tangible encounters that work best for you. This can require some experimentation. As you use various faculties, note how rapidly your feelings of anxiety drop. Also, be as exact as could reasonably be expected. What is the particular sound or kind of development that influences you the most? For instance, in case you're a music sweetheart, tune into various specialists and sorts of music until you discover the tune that in a split second lifts and loosens up you.

Investigate an assortment of tangible encounters with the goal that regardless of where you are, you'll have a device to mitigate pressure.

The models recorded underneath are planned to be a bouncing off point. Let your creative mind run free and think of extra things to attempt. At the point when you locate the privilege of tactile strategy, you'll know it.

Sight. Take a gander at a valued photograph, or a most loved token. Use a plant or blossoms to breathe life into your workspace. Appreciate the excellence of nature: a nursery, the seashore, a recreation center, or your own lawn. Encircle yourself with hues that lift your spirits. Close your eyes and picture a spot that feels tranquil and reviving.

Smell. Light a scented flame or consume some incense. Examination with various basic oils. Take in the pleasant ambiance or another kind of bloom. Appreciate, spotless, natural air. Spritz on your preferred aroma or cologne.

Contact. Enclose yourself by a warm cover. Pet a canine or feline. Hold a consoling article (a plush toy, a most loved keepsake). Give yourself a hand or neck need. Wear attire that feels delicate against your skin.

Taste. Gradually enjoying a most loved treat can unwind, yet thoughtless eating will just add to your pressure and your waistline. The key is to enjoy your feeling of taste carefully and with some restraint. Bite a bit of sugarless gum. Enjoy a little of dull chocolate. Taste a steaming mug of espresso or tea or an invigorating virus drink. Eat a ready bit of natural product. Appreciate a sound, crunchy nibble (celery, carrots, or trail blend).

Development. If you will shut down when you're under pressure or have encountered injury, stress-ease exercises that make you move might be especially useful. Run set up or bounce around. Move around. Stretch or roll your head around and around. Take a short walk. Crush a rubbery pressure ball.

Sound. Sing or play a most loved tune. Tune into quiet or inspiring music. Check out the soundtrack of nature-smashing waves, the breeze stirring the trees, fowls singing. Purchase a little wellspring, so you can appreciate the mitigating sound of running water in your home or office. Hang wind rolls almost through an open window.

Tip 4: Find tactile motivation

Experiencing difficulty recognizing tactile procedures that work for you? Search for motivation around you, from your sights as you approach your day to recollections from quite a while ago.

Recollections. Recollect what you did as a kid to quiet down. On the off chance that you had a cover or stuffed toy, you may profit by material incitement. Take a stab at tying a finished scarf around your neck before an arrangement or keeping a bit of delicate softened cowhide in your pocket.

Watch others. Seeing how others manage pressure can give you important knowledge. Baseball players regularly pop gum before going fixing to make something happen. Artists regularly talk up the group before performing. Ask individuals you know how they remain centered under tension.

Guardians. Recollect what your folks never really off stream. Did your mom feel more loose after a long walk? Accomplished your dad work in the yard in the wake of a monotonous day?

<u>The intensity of the creative mind</u>. When drawing upon your tactile tool stash becomes propensity, attempt essentially envisioning distinctive sensations when stress strikes. The memory of your endearing face's will have a similar quieting or invigorating consequences for your mind as observing her photograph. At the point when you can review a solid sensation, you'll never be without a fast pressure help instrument.

Tip 5: Make brisk pressure alleviation a propensity

It is difficult to use your faculties in a smaller than usual-or not all that minor-emergency. From the start, it will feel simpler to simply surrender, to wait and worry. With time, calling upon your faculties will be natural. Think about the procedure like figuring out how to drive or play golf. You don't ace the aptitude in one exercise; you need to rehearse until it turns out to be natural. You'll feel you're overlooking something on the off chance that you don't tune into your body during testing times. Here's the way to make it a propensity.

<u>Start a little</u>. Rather than testing your fast pressure, alleviation apparatuses on a wellspring of significant pressure, start with an expected low-level wellspring of stress, such as preparing supper toward the finish of a tough day or plunking down to take care of tabs.

<u>Recognize and target</u>. Consider only one low-level stressor you realize will happen a few times each week, for example, driving. Promise to focus on that stressor with speedy pressure alleviation without fail. Following half a month, focus on a subsequent stressor, etc.

<u>Test drive tangible information</u>. If you are rehearsing snappy pressure help on your drive to work, carry a scented cloth with you one day, attempt music one more day, and attempt a development the following day. Continue testing until you locate a reasonable champ.

<u>Experiment with the procedure</u>. With something doesn't work, don't constrain it. Proceed onward until you find what works best for you. It ought to be pleasurable and perceptibly quieting.

<u>Discussing about it</u>. Enlightening companions or relatives regarding the pressure alleviation techniques you're testing will assist you with incorporating them into your life. If that wasn't already enough, will undoubtedly begin a fascinating discussion: everybody identifies with the subject of pressure.

Tip 6: Practice any place you are

The best piece of tactile based techniques is the mindfulness that you have control. Regardless of where you are or what you're doing, speedy pressure help is inside arm's scope.

Fast pressure helps at home

<u>Engaging</u>. Forestall pre-party butterflies by playing vivacious music. Light candles, the glimmer and aroma will invigorate your faculties. Wear garments that cause you to feel loose and sure.

<u>Kitchen</u>. Straightforwardness kitchen worry by taking in the fragrance of each fixing. Take pleasure in the fragile surface of an eggshell. Value the heaviness of an onion.

<u>Youngster and connections</u>. Forestall losing your cool during a spousal altercation by pressing the tips of your thumb and index finger together. At the point when your little child has a fit of rage, rub moisturizer into your hands and taken in the aroma.

<u>Don't combine work with your behavior, stress will end</u>. In today's era, we have been given such a layer of decency and humility, under which we are often unable to say. We often take more work pressure on ourselves. And when incomplete, we get stressed. To avoid this, take the work according to your strength and tackle it.

Chapter-15: Power of Positive Thoughts and Belief

"Happiness is when what you think, what you say, and what you do are in harmony" – *Mahatma Gandhi.*

This is how some people have everything, yet they are not happy. There are many people who have wealth, have a successful career, have an excellent life partner and have good friends, still they remain hopeless and unhappy. And on the other side there are people who are poor and unhappy and not physically fit, they have nothing. People who face every problem yet are happy in their life but are the reason for thinks difference.

What did you like in it? The answer is that how do you look at your life. What happens if you have an awful accident in your life? Have you been thinking about the negative aspect or came out of the situation thinking positive? We understand it with a story famous comedian John Belushi in the 1970s during his time he did memorable shows and was counted among the best entertainers. Belushi achieved great popularity at 22. He bought a property in New York and married a beautiful girl.

He had everything yet they were not happy, he was alone from inside. He resorted to drugs to overcome this loneliness. He died of a drugs overdose at just 33 years old. And the other story is W. Michelle's has an accident in which he is completely injured. But he does not give up and after recover continue his business but one day he has another accident.

The plane he was travelling on crashed, which paralyzed him down to his waist. But Michelle shows him passion to live again instead of sad, started business again and become a billionaire before he married and lived a joyful life. So always fill your brain with positive thoughts and take the right action and communicate with yourself to maintain positive behavior.

<u>The power of state.</u> Our mind has 2 state one is enabling state who gives us strength, make capable. This happens when your mind is filled with happiness, love, strength and confidence. Second state is paralyzing. It happens when your mind is filled with sadness, scary doubt, despair and worry. You have a lot of power from this paralysis state. You have the power to control your brain. You can create this enabling state at your own will.

The birth of excellence belief. When we hear words like faith and trust, we connect it with religion. Belief is not the word of religion and books. It gives us direction and guides in life, and this is your perspective to see the world. Our belief gives order to our nervous system when you believe in something. It becomes true; it gives you the power of take action. Pablo Salas was a skilled musician and played many musical instruments with the piano.

At 90, he suffered from arthritis and emphysema, his hand was swollen and fingers started turning and he also trouble breathing. But when he played the piano the swelling of his fingers would disappear and he would never have trouble breathing his deep faith in music

had treated him with illness. That is called a
power of belief.

Chapter -16: Tips for Control Your Anger

Do you smoke when someone bites you in traffic? Is your blood pressure rocket when your child refuses to cooperate? Anger is a normal and even healthy emotion, but it is essential to deal with it positively. Uncontrolled anger can weigh on both your health and your relationships. Ready to get your passion under control? Chronic anger that flares up all the time or spiral out of control can have serious on the following:-

1. **<u>Physical health</u>**. Constantly operating at high levels of stress and anger makes you more susceptible to heart disease, diabetes, a weakened immune system, insomnia, and high blood pressure.

2. **<u>Mental health</u>**. Chronic anger consumes huge amounts of mental energy, and clouds your thinking, making it can also lead to stress, depression, and other mental health problems.

3.   **Career**. Constructive criticism, creative differences, and heated debate can be healthy. But lashing out only alienates your colleagues, supervisors, or clients and erodes their respect.

4.   **Relationships**. Anger can cause lasting scars in the people you love most and get in the way of friendships and work relationships. Explosive anger makes it hard for others to trust you, speak honestly, or feel comfortable and is especially damaging to children.

These are the nine anger management tips.

1. **Think before you speak**. At the moment's heat, it is easy to say that you will regret it later. Take a few moments to collect your thoughts before you say anything and allow others involved in the situation to do the same.

2. **Once you calm down, express your anger**. As soon as you are thinking, express your frustration in a vocal but non-relevant way. Try to control your concerns and needs and directly without telling others or controlling them.

3. **<u>Do some exercises</u>**. Physical activity can help reduce the stress that can make you angry. If you feel your anger increasing, go for brisk walking or running, or spend some time doing other enjoyable physical activities.

4. **<u>Take a timeout</u>**. Timeouts are not just for children. Give yourself brief breaks during the day, which is stressful. A few moments of quiet time can help you feel better prepared to move forward without getting irritated or angry.

5. **<u>Identify solutions</u>**. Instead of focusing on the thing that has made you mad, work on solving the issue at hand. Does your child's messy room drive you crazy? Close the door. Does your partner come late for dinner every night? Schedule a meal later in the evening or agree to eat on your own a few times a week. Remind yourself that anger will cure nothing and can only make it worse.

6. **<u>Stay with 'I' Statements</u>**. To avoid having criticism or blame, which can only increase stress, use 'I' statements to describe the problem. Be respected and distinguished, for

example, say, 'I am upset that you never work without the consonant'.

7. **There is not a catch**. Forgiveness is a powerful tool. If you allow anger and other negative feelings to exclude positive emotions, you can swallow yourself with your bitterness or sense of injustice. But if you can forgive someone who offended you, you can probably learn from the situation and strengthen your relationship.

8. **Use humor to release stress**. Being lighter can help to spread fear. Use humor to help you cope with the anger you are experiencing and, possibly, any unrealistic expectations that you have about how things should go. Avoid satire, though, it can hurt feelings and make things worse.

9. **Practice relaxation skills**. When your anger flares up, put relaxation skills to work. Practice deep breathing exercises, visualize a relaxing scene, or repeat a clam word or phrase, such as 'take it easy'. You can also listen to music, write in a magazine, or do some yoga, whatever it takes to encourage relaxation.

Chapter -17: How to Stop the Problem of Overthinking

"The key to being happy is knowing you have the power to choose what to accept and what to let go" –Dodinsky.

Thoughts are powerful. Your thoughts become your reality. As Tony Robbins says, "Whatever you hold in your mind on a consistent basis is exactly what you will experience in your life." This is something that the world's most successful people realize and the only difference between them and everyone else is that they have learned how to harness the power of thoughts to help them achieve. The classic overthinking definition is, "to think about something too much or for too long."

Those who keep thinking something all the time or have a problem of overthinking must listen to one line that overthinking is deteriorating their lives. Do you know a scientific fact, 'those who think normally, their brain works well and those who think more have a low IQ'.

Whether you are a student or an adult doing a job, you must have a problem of overthinking. In today's world, hardly anyone would be in peace. You always keep thinking something; is it right? When you think about one thing, another thought, on the other side, comes into your mind and it keeps bothering you. If you are a student, you will have a tension of study, if you are doing a job, you will have a tension of a job and you must be always thinking something because of all these things.

As per the science, overthinking is making you more weak; deteriorating your life. In many studies of Stanford, the scientists have come to know on the scientific basis that overthinking keeps reducing the creativity power of our mind and makes slow its growth. To think more than normal decreases the efficiency of your neurons. You must know the solution of all these problems of overthinking.

There is a story that will change your life completely. You would listen to a very surprising and true story. It will change your thinking altogether.

There was a magician named Abdul Kadar who claimed, if he was locked in a cell, he would prove himself within one hour by unlocking its doors and getting out of it. Many employees of small cells summoned Kadar the cell, but he would get out every time without a key. Even no one knew how he would do it. Everyone just noticed that he would keep a long and flexible steel wire beneath his belt and he, maybe, would put the wire into the lock and open it with a magical trick. But a person can't open all the locks with just a single steel wire or without using a key. Opened one lock, okay. But, with only a wire, he would successfully unlock the doors of all the cells where he was confined in and slowly became famous because of his this skill. Then, the employees of a large cell heard Kadar's stories about how he would get out within one hour after locking him in any cell. One employee of the cell said, 'I will make him experience of the world's most dangerous cell door, one such a cell that no one can open'. They challenged Kadar to come and prove himself by getting out of their cell within one hour. One day, they fixed and even Kadar accepted the challenge. They stared at the event before many people.

Kadar ready for the magic. A guard standing there called him with applause. Kadar entered the cell with a great confidence. Then, the guard standing there called him and said with a low voice. This is the strongest and advance cell door of the entire world. Having heard it, his confidence level became a little less. But still he felt that he would unlock it too with his magic trick. The door was locked and then it was the time for Kadar to show his magic. He opened his belt and drew a large iron pin out of it. The pin was his only actual weapon, which he would put below the lock of the cell door and unlocked it. He would always hide the pin. Kadar put it into the lock and started trying to break it. Everyone was fully sure that he would unlock the cell door easily within one hour, he had opened many locks. But what the guard of the cell said was still in his mind.

However, he started his task and unlocking the cell door. After thirty minutes, the confidence he had slowly faded out. One hour later, his entire face was full of sweat. However, he couldn't still open the lock. Two hours passed, he still could not unlock the door of the cell. He gave up after two-and-a-half hours. He got angry and hit the door with his hands. He saw that they never locked the door of the cell. That's why he was confused in the mechanism of the lock. But, on the other side, the guard had even told him that it was the best lock of the country and therefore, he was caught in something that was not real. The door was already unlocked. The guard had told Kadar before the competition that it was the best lock of the country. What the guard said, was fixed in his mind and so, he was overthinking about such a thing that did not exist.

As per the scientific researches, there are around seventy thousand (70000) different thoughts in the mind of a person in a day and ninety-five percent (95%) out of seventy thousand (70,000) thoughts are useless, you even overthinking about such unnecessary things that are actually not problem too at all. As well you can't focus on your goals just like Kadar. Someone like the guard says something to you and you keep overthinking about it. You keep ruining your life because of overthinking.

What is there in your life? Do you feel you can't do whatever there is in your life? How many times would it be happening to you in life in which the solution's simple? You make easy task difficult overthinking in your life as Kadar did. If he had seen the lock of the cell door carefully just before starting, he probably would not have borne the insult that day and thus, he had to face such a lock was in his mind. There is an American proverb, 'when there is no enemy inside you, the enemy from outside can't even touch you'.

If you clear the doubts you have and increase your confidence, no one can spoil you. Brain is very helpful for you, but it will support you as much as, on the other side, will tell you a lie. Then what to do? Keep confidence in yourself and not to think more than well as to keep doing your work because Kadar has shown that whatever locks are, they are just in your mind.

There are no locks in this world that you can't unlock. You can do anything and if you are feeling you can do one thing and can't do another one, you really believe such untruthful things. These untruthful things or barriers are just set in your mind. There is a quote, 'think less, live better, think less, live more'. You must follow it if you want to enjoy a good life. Do daydreaming, because it increases your intelligence more. Think, but think about only good things throughout the day that affect positive in your life. The good things can't never be overthinking. Positive thinking destroys overthinking i.e., if you think positively about something, you will always away from overthinking. If you think much about positive things, you will get energy instead of having a headache.

A positive 'aura' is around those people who think positively. You look at someone attractive because this positive 'aura' is present around him or her. You might have noticed, thinking too much is the problem when a wrong and negative thought come into your mind. Your 'aura' will increase as much as you will think positively about something and you will be more attractive towards the people because of positivity. But the most of the thoughts throughout the day bother you.

You think little about the things like love and happiness. You don't overthink about how much this world is beautiful. A good thing can never be a problem. The second root of overthinking is actually your identity, i.e., your ego. Once look valuation your life at your childhood photo in the album. You will see a smile in your face or yourself playing. Compare how you were in childhood and what you have been now. You will come to know, you think less when you are at the stage of childhood and as you think less, you are happy.

The fact is that thinking is necessary, but to some extent. Without thinking, no work can be done. Without evaluation, your life is useless. Yes, it is necessary to examine how your life is going on; but don't think too much. Even to make balance your mind is very necessary. You should never be ego on yourself because later on, it turns into overthinking. The less you boast and the more you are full of smile and happy, the more people will be attractive towards you. Don't wait for the condition being right; make yourself right.

The typical mentality is, when everything is okay in life or you get a good job, you will be right and everything will be right. But the actual thing is just opposite to it. First, make yourself right; then after, the things of your life will be right. When you improve yourself or work on yourself, your life is good for itself. If you have to think, think good things and work on them. You overthink because you control the things of the world without becoming perfect. First, make yourself perfect; work on yourself; make yourself awesome; then, the things of the world will start to be perfect automatically. Learn to live now.

Sometimes, it seems how good the childhood was: how interesting the school life was; wish the good olden golden days are back! Whether you do anything, the old days will not come back i.e., the old days will not supposed to return back whether the good days or the bad days have passed. So, you need to leave the past. If you think or keep overthinking about whatever you have made mistakes in the past, you will not able to move further or never move further in your life. If you have made a big mistake in the past, accept it and say to your mind that you have changed now. I, maybe, have told you before too, 'focus on one thing'. But, the most of the problems in your life occur when you start managing many things together. Whatever you have to do in life, first focus on one thing; become specialized on it and devote your full energy to it. This is the best idea to keep yourself away from overthinking. It makes the followings:-

1. Create unnecessary suffering in your life.

2. Lead you to waste a lot of time and energy.

3. Make you feel bad, and

4. Lead you to feel overwhelmed.

Chapter -18: How to Increase the Power of Thinking

"Train your mind to see the good in everything. Positivity is a choice. The happiness of your life depends on the quality of your thoughts".

There is an expanded mindset about the importance of one's well-being, and people talk about it openly. Here are some basis for your mental health which will give you shot every day. Reduce time over web-based media networking. It has long been ringing in our ears.

An attempt to appreciate the less enjoyable moments of your life about the things you think you're getting a big chance based on the featured snapshots of others you're running through web-based network media. It's important that you sleep. Practice before bedtime every day. It gives the brain signals, which is an ideal opportunity to relax, and you usually switch off the node.

Evite any interruption by computer and eat light at night before hitting the hay. The reminder of a good evening will allow you to continue the next morning again. Start the day early. It gives you the opportunity to follow your own habits-prayers, meditation and exercise before you go to work. This way you can unpack and set up yourself to bed when you get back from work. It gives you a feeling of satisfaction which is making the most of the day. Also, having a full night's rest helps. Advanced year expression is self-preservation. Also, the sample is definitely searching for a long time, at the off chance you'd like to mark it.

A hot shower can be the best observation tool you can turn on the web, while relaxing music. Stay the same, the key thing is figuring out what you want most to do and helping you to relax. It can fly, analyze a book, cook and so on. Keep your food habits on a list. That is not even after running the network. Make sure you swallow the food that will give you the essential ingredients. Replace your eating regimen with regular exercise, to be truly and intellectually. Self-medication is an obvious remedy. There's nothing more reliable than self-healing ascribed to many natural forms of healing. Natural medicine usually takes the form of herbs and other similarities to nature. Self- healing is very different in that one agrees to heal with no herb by natural means.

Chapter -19: How Can We Increase Concentration Power

"You deserve to be happy. You deserve to live a life you are excited about. Don't let others make you forget that".

Human mind is not meant to work in chaos. Our senses are prone to easy distractions, with our concentration breaking with a slight buzz in any aspect of our atmosphere. Someone plays a song in distance, we get distracted; someone texts, we get distracted; someone chats, we get distracted; no one does anything, we still get distracted. That's how weak our concentration span is.

The following ways will help you to increase to build happiness through concentration power.

How to increase concentration. As we know, for getting anything in life, our focus or concentration takes to play the main role. People, who have scattered minds, cannot achieve any happiness/success in life, because their mind works everywhere so focus is not there, concentration has vanished, so what you expect in this situation, what you can get, in fact, you are in a total loss. Without concentration on a single subject, you cannot do any big thing in this area. So either, you are a student, professional, or whatever you do, always keep in mind, concentration is the main key to completing your tasks.

Common factor on concentration affects. We all are living a busy life in all the ways, so it is a natural thing if we lose our concentration, but you should understand this is not your issue of every human being which is living in this world so, how successful people are motivated all the time? They are living in the same world, in which, I and you are living, so the main thing is your determination to understand, be concentrated in every kind of situation.

People lose their job or they are jobless, they failed in business, their income is low, these factors are the reasons of demotivation and of course, you lose your concentration due to your frustration of failure, but again I repeat, there is no other option, except this, you need to be motivated and the best way to keep motivated himself, is rapid action on a certain task which you want to do.

How can we motivated. As I described in the above line, you need to make busy yourself in positive activities, note down your daily tasks, and get started, this is the best way of getting rid of scattered thoughts. When you will be busy or doing some work, then you unconsciously are, being motivated. So keep busy yourself according to the nature of your work so you will not also be motivated all the time, but also your concentration will be increased.

Fail to achieve concentration. If you spend your days without doing anything, I mean you are an idle guy or girl or woman, and then you lose your concentration with your own hands because your idle mind creates a different kind of useless theories and you would make yourself confused among of them. The result will be zero. So, you need to make yourself busy with your work. You need to ignore useless activities: they have no gain or benefit.

Summary.   Concentration is everything so, always being busy with positive daily tasks. As a result, you will not have time to spend your energy on useless thoughts. When you are doing some work or task, and then try to make focus on a certain thing and ignore every other stressful thought. Very Soon, you will see your life is changing and that change will create a great positive impact on every sector of your life.

Chapter -20: How to Stop Procrastination

"Happiness comes when we stop complaining about the troubles we have and offer thanks for all the troubles we don't have".

Quotes for procrastination written by various legends are given below:-

You may delay, but time will not,

and lost time is never found again

*-**Benjamin Franklin***

Procrastination is the thief of time,

collar him- ***Charles Dickens***

In delay, then lies no plenty –

William Shakespeare

Only put off until tomorrow, what

*undone– **Pablo Picasso***

Procrastination is a trap that many of us fall into. In fact, according to researcher and speaker Piers Steel, 95 percent of us procrastinate to some degree. While it may be comforting to know that you're not alone, it can be sobering to realize just how much it can hold you back. Procrastination is often confused with laziness, but they are very different.

<u>Fear of get Disapproved</u>. Don't fear of getting disapproved, think positive. How you think and feel about yourself is called self-esteem. It is important to achieve the success in your life. Self-acceptance is the important thing in your life because you need to accept your first. You think I am so black; I am too fat; I am too short. Accept yourself change your weakness into strength. If you lose your self- esteem you get fear and you depressed you lose your hope in your life so whatever situation you faced don't lose your self- esteem. It is the key to the happiness and success.

<u>Fear of get overwhelmed</u>. Most of us are in fear of getting overwhelmed. We think our work is too hard we can't do this it's too hard we think. If you have too heavy work use reverse calendar method.

Pain of Displeasure. We can see kids they play games do something as they like but they not to be lazy because they like the work and doing. If kids are to study, they get to lazy or they procrastinate because we are project the education like a serious think that only kids get pain in education or displeasure. Student education like fun thing not to be pain. So you guys love the work of what you doing, it gives you a pleasure you don't procrastinate the work.

F ace

E verything

A nd

R ise

Fear and failures. Most of us we think I need to start own business but we don't do or we procrastinate it because it not as standard income if you going to a normal job you need to start a side business. You to do the side business regularly which the business gets standard then you quit the job as you like. If you need to get out of your failures, create a safe zone. Fear and failure are stop the action what we taking.

Too much of fear and failure to take the action faster. When the problem is too heavy, we are taking our action faster than the previous one. Create a safe zone to you achieve safeguard yourself from the problem. Don't procrastinate situation what you face it and finish it. Love the work what you doing. Improve your self - esteem to achieve the success and happy in the life.

<u>Summary</u>. Procrastination is the habit of delaying an important task, usually by focusing on less urgent, more enjoyable, and easier activities instead. It is different from laziness, which is the unwillingness to act.

Procrastination can restrict your potential and undermine your career. It can also disrupt teamwork, reduce morale, and even lead to depression and job loss. So, it's crucial to take proactive steps to prevent it.

The first step to overcoming procrastination is to recognize that you're doing it. Then, identify the reasons behind your behavior and use appropriate strategies to manage and overcome it.

Chapter -21: Falling Into the Battlefield

"A mind always employed is always happy. This is the true secret, the grand recipe, for felicity" – Thomas Jefferson.

Who doesn't want to succeed in life? Everyone wants to live their life according to their dreams and enjoy all kinds of luxuries. But we that not everyone succeeds. Someone celebrates victory, someone suffers the humiliation of defeat. When the joyous of success comes to someone, the sorrow of failure comes. In this race of life, where we see successful people living a joyful life, we also see unsuccessful people crying over their destiny. Have you ever wondered why?

In fact, the lives of successful people are very organized and they achieve their goals by overcoming the problems and obstacles that come in the way because of good planning, while the unsuccessful people fail because of their lack of planning and waste of time. We give the causes of these failures and their solutions below:-

<u>Enthusiasm is essential</u>. Most young people, when setting their goals, rarely show the dedication and enthusiasm required to achieve their goals. Usually the desires are to make a lot of money, to build a new house, to reach a certain position or status, to expand the business, to buy a new car, and so on. But because of a lack of determination, even minor obstacles can become overwhelming.

In such a case, it is important to and dedications yourself with this goal in your eyes and feel the taste of success. This is the moment that makes you want to move forward again. Then with hard work, enthusiasm and dedication you try to achieve your goal and you succeed. With determination, young people nurture every destination, even the stars, while the lack of moral wastes the hard work.

<u>Fear of failure.</u> *"Failure should be our teacher, not our undertaker. Failure is delay, not defeat. It is a temporary detour, not a dead* *end. Failure is something we can avoid only by saying nothing, doing nothing, and being nothing"-Denis Watiley.* People afraid of falling fail because they do not know how to deal with the obstacles and dangers that come with achieving their goals. And the fear of failure rides on their heads. For example, sometimes we avoid getting a job in a fresh place and leaving the old job even though we get a wonderful offer, lest I leave my job and I am not satisfied there, I don't know; I have better responsibilities there.

In the same way, when starting a new business, choosing a subject in the field or education or at the beginning of their professional life, many young people fall prey to unnecessary fears. This fear is a temporary thought. To move forward, one has to get out of its clutches and accept the realities of life. Not everything in the world is to our liking. In the same way, success and failure sometimes comes with it. But turning defeat into victory is the actual battle, and that is the secret of success.

<u>Fear of success</u>. After achieving success, most people become afraid to trust anyone. Sometimes they think people can deceive them. Because of their fear, they cannot focus on their business and fall into the trap of selfishness and self-deception. Fear of failure because it weakens your emotions, ambitions and dedication. For example, you have amassed immense wealth. Now if negative thoughts confine you to this siege like, if this wealth could not make me happy, not related to any accident or trouble, if I looked, the family would start burning me then what will happen. This kind of negative thinking also weakens the intentions of a determined young person. So replace negative thoughts with positive ones. For example, decide that I am happy and I will be happy. Whatever the problems, I will solve them and with this success I will also help my circle of friends and family.

<u>Unreal timetable</u>. Most young people set unrealistic time goals to achieve their goal. For example, I will do this in a week and reach this place in a year. But when the goal of the week is not met, they fall and become discouraged.

While small failures are the stepping stone to great success. Achieving goals by realistically allocating time realistically never fails and always be flexible when planning. That goal doesn't have to be achieved within the time. You set.

There are several factors such as poor health, poor condition, poor outages. Also, if our work is connected to some other people, make a schedule keeping that in mind. Stay calm and achieve your goal with sincerity, dedication and hard work. Never be discouraged by a failure but keen trying and try to learn from the experiences of failure by taking them positively. Start over with a constant struggle. Review your work repeatedly. Don't repeat mistakes, but remember them.

<u>Never give up</u>. Filled with self-doubt, many people are prepared to give up. Sometimes we get discouraged by a temporary failure, and thus we find it impossible to achieve our goal. For example, in a field we get admission in higher education. After success in the first one or two semesters, when the next semester results in a drop in quality, the youngster is usually discouraged. Michael Phelps, World Swimmer, who achieved 08 Olympic medals, when his doctor recommended not to take part in the Olympic due to his hand got fracture. But he never gives up, practiced swimming without using his hand and he made the world record. He proved the success and defeated his doctor advice. We all know that 'a winner never quits and a quitter never wins'.

Chapter -22: How to Build a Positive Attitude

"The belief that youth is the happiest time of life is founded on a fallacy. The happiest person is the person who thinks the most interesting thoughts, and we grow happier as we grow older" – William Phelps.

If you want to build and maintain a positive attitude, you need to consciously practice the following methods:

Step 1- Change focus, look for the Positive

You need to become a seeker of good. You need to focus on the positive in your life. Start looking for what is right in a person or situation instead of looking for what is wrong. Because of our conditioning, most of us are so attitude to finding fault and looking for what is wrong that we often forget to see what's positive.

<u>**Some people always look at the negative side. Who is a pessimist?**</u>

- Pessimists are moaners, groaners and permanent complainers.
- Aura unhappy when they have no troubles to speak of.
- Feel bad when they have to feel good, for fear they will feel worse when they feel better.
- Always switch off the lights to see how dark it is.
- Cannot enjoy their health today because they think they may be sick tomorrow.
- Not only expect the worst, but to make the worst of whatever happens.
- Don't see the doughnut, they only see the hole.
- Forget their blessings and count their troubles.
- Know what hard work hurts no one but believe 'take a chance?'.
- Be an Optimist.

Be so strong that nothing can disturb your peace of mind. Talk about health, happiness and prosperity to every person you meet. Make all your friends feel that you appreciate their pleasant qualities and strengths. Look at the sunny side of everything. Think only of the best, work only for the best, and expect only the best. The success of others as you are about your own, forget the mistakes of the past and pressed onto the outstanding achievements of the future. Give everyone a smile, spend so much time improving yourself that you have no time left to criticize others. Be too big for worry and to Nobel for anger.

<u>**Step 2 : Make a Habit of Doing it Now**</u>.

Don't fortunate part of life is as Oliver Wendell Holmes said, 'Most people go to their Graves, with music still in them.' We don't achieve excellence because of our own lack of vision.

We have all procrastinated or another in our lives. I know I have, only to have regretted in later. Procrastination leads to a negative attitude. The reverse is just as true. They feed on each other. The habit of procrastination fatigue more than the effort it takes to do the task.

A completed task is fulfilling and energizing: an incomplete task drains energy. If you want to build and maintain a positive attitude, get into the habit of living in the present and doing it now.

<u>Step 3 : Develop an Attitude of Gratitude</u>.

Gratitude reflects humility. It keeps a person on ground. It is a great philosophy to live by, forget what others have done for you and never remember what you have done for others'. Count your blessing, not your troubles. It is not uncommon to hear that someone, because of an accident, became blind or paralyzed, what got a million dollars in a settlement from the insurance company. How many of us would like to trade places with that person? We are so focused on complaining about things we do not have that we lost sight of the things we have. There is a lot to be thankful for.

When I say count your blessings, not your troubles, I don't mean that a person should become complacent. If complaisance was the message you got, I would be guilty of miscommunication and you of selective listening.

It hides many of our blessings treasures–count your blessings, not your troubles.

Chapter -23: Why Don't More People Set Goals?

"When one door of happiness closes, another opens; but often we look so long at the closed door that we do not see the one which has opened for us" – Helen Keller.

The man who tries to do something and fail are infinite Lee better than those who try to do nothing and succeed. - Lloyd Jones.

There are many reasons people don't set goals, they are:-

1. **A pessimistic attitude**. Looking for the pitfalls rather than the possibilities.

2. **Fear of failure**. Thinking, 'what if I don't make it?' Subconsciously people feel that if they don't set goals and don't achieve them, they feel they have not failed, they don't realize that they

have failed to begin with by not having any goals.

3. **<u>Fear of success</u>**. A low self- image of fear of having to live up to their success causes some people to fear success.

4. **<u>A lack of ambition</u>**. Power of limited thinking prevents us from progress. There was a fisherman who, every time he caught an enormous fish, and would throw it back into the river, keeping on with the smaller ones. A man watching this unusual behavior was the fisherman why he was doing this. The fisherman replied, "because I have a small frying pan". Most people never make it big in life because they are carrying a small frying pan. That is limited thinking.

5. **<u>A fear of rejection</u>**. Worrying that, "if I don't make it, what will other people say?"

6. **<u>Procrastination</u>**. Thinking "someday, I will set my goals". This ties in with a lack of ambition.

7. **Low self-esteem**. Because to be a person is not internally driven and has no inspiration.

8. **Ignorance of the importance of goals**. Nobody taught them and they never learnt the importance of goal setting.

9. **Lack of knowledge about goal setting**. People don't know the mechanics of setting goals. They need a step-by-step guide so they can follow a system.

Goals Must Be Balanced. Our life is like a wheel with 6 spokes as given below:-

1. **Family**. Our loved ones, the reason to live and make a living.

2. **Financial**. Represents our career and the things that money can buy.

3. **Physical**. Without good health, nothing makes sense.

4. **Mental**. This represents knowledge and wisdom.

5. **<u>Social</u>**. Every individual and organization has a social responsibility, without which society dies.

6. **<u>Spiritual</u>**. Your value system represents ethics and character.

In any of these sports is out of alignment, your life goes out of balance. Take a few minutes to just consider if any of these 6 spokes were missing, what would your life be like.

Chapter -24: How Can Find the Happiness

Who doesn't want to be happy? Everyone seeks the meaning of happiness in their life or the key to happiness. Actually, the key to happiness is to be happy.

Without realizing it, you only depend on the outside to make you happy. However, you need not be pessimistic, because being happy is an ability that can be trained.

What is the key to happiness in life?

Implementing the key to happiness is a continuous process and needs to be trained every day. You cannot expect that you will be happy from time to time. Here are some 'keys to happiness' that you can try.

<u>Choose Happiness</u>. The key to happiness is near to you, because being happy is a life option. The key to happiness does not always come from outside, such as winning the lottery, becoming rich, and so on.

Sometimes, you feel that you do not deserve that happiness and inadvertently engage in behaviors that really make you sad. Tell yourself that you want to be happy from now on.

Fighting Negative feelings and thoughts. Unknowingly, negative thoughts and feelings can overwhelm your heart and mind and make you sad. Recognizing and eliminating these negative patterns is the key to happiness.

When these negative feelings and thoughts arise, challenge the negative feelings and thoughts by asking yourself if they really are. Another way is to stop thinking and feeling the negative things that are being experienced.

Deal with stress. Stress is always in life, but don't let stress make you less happy. Deal with stress by doing comfortable things like meditation, yoga, hobbies, etc.

<u>Take time for self-reflection</u>. Just don't engage in your work, give yourself free time or give me time. Use my time to think about the things that have happened in your life and how you can improve.

<u>To be grateful</u>. Realizing happiness and expressing gratitude is the key to happiness. Problems happen every day, but being grateful for what you have realized makes you feel that life is not as bad as imagined and still you have a lot of things to make yourself happy.

<u>Write a daily journal</u>. A journal or diary is a tool that can find out what was felt and thought, and to remember the good things that happened in that one day. You can find the key to happiness through the things that are happening around you daily.

<u>Make a note of happiness</u>. Like a magazine, you can write or write a list of good things that make you feel happy or grateful. For example, remembering that someone helped you lift thing, and so on.

<u>Forgive others</u>. Holding on to anger and anger can reduce the feeling of happiness you have. Forgiving someone else is not as easy as turning your hand, but catching a complaint will not give the person who hurts you.

Feeling angry at other people only makes you sad. Slowly try to forgive that person and forgive the other person by sympathizing with the mistakes they have made the thing.

Chapter -25: Independent Ability Will Define Your Identity

"The secret to happiness is freedom ... And the secret to freedom is courage" – *Thucydides.*

If you lost your job, don't be scared or panic. You are not the only one who did this happened with you. Many people all over the world are experiencing the same thing right now.

Accept yourself and experience it. You need to learn something from your little things. Our first task is to understand the meaning of your life, what is important and what is not. We need to give important to ourselves. Puzzle and fun games can entertain, but not an entire day for a while.

Use your time effectively and even make this phase of your life in a positive. Give yourself a chance if you feel that you have made a mistake, forgive yourself for that and accept the things you have and learn new things that will enhance your resume.

Lockdown is not forever. After this lockdown, everyone will start a new life. For this new life, there are a lot of things that you can learn by staying home. If you are a newbie, then start from zero and raise your risks and put your full efforts to complete every task.

Cooking classes. With so much free time available in your hands. Now is the ideal time to test your skills with those recipes and ingredients you have not tried before. There are you-tube and other websites where you can share your unique recipes. Everyone is trying to learn something new in this valuable time where you can be creative in the kitchen and try cooking yourself and not take away all the time.

Yoga. It is a traditional routine to nourish the brain, body, and soul. Celebrate your every day with yoga moves. It calms your mind and refreshes you from inside. It gives you a positive outlook towards life and drives away negative thoughts and helps you to a better life. Inhale your positive attitude and exhale your devil part. It makes you superfluous.

<u>Upwork and freelancer</u>. Up work or freelancer both platform give you online work whether it is a data entry work or website work if you are good at PP, Dot Net, Java, Word Press, HMTL languages, and the Microsoft office then you can do any work online and offline. They are open sources and will give you work that definitely it reflects as earning.

You can earn as much as you can here and make yourself independent.

<u>Article and blogs</u>. If you are good in English and have a great command, then you can write your article and blog and publish it easily. It will help you grow yourself. Blogs are where you have to buy your own domain name, after that, you will create a website and after visiting you can add your blogs. This does not happen in the articles, write any article of your choice (must be unique) and put it on any article website they will pay account to how many people spend their precious time to read them.

Dance. Dance is a great art. It makes you feel calm and energetic all day. There are lots of varieties of Zumba, Salsa, break-dance, kathak, etc. Dancing whatever has happened during my day in a week, I can leave it behind and I put my ballet shoes on. It increases your confidence if you have stage fear or hesitation. You can dance to boost yourself. It feels more pleasurable and enthusiastic. It is a very common theme in all the entire countries.

Gardening. Growing your own beautiful flowers and plants can also feel equal a reward and pleasure, to bring a touch of class and beauty to your home, interior, and garden. You can add different amazing plants and increase the value of your balcony. Also, you can design it according to your taste. You can move dead spots, rotted stems, and insects and easily escalate to your healthy plants.

Reading Books. Reading books is a good way to kill your free time. It is a way to relax and reduce stress and scratch the brain for healthy functioning. You can gain a unique knowledge by going nowhere. Books are your fast friend and never begrudge with your success.

New Language. Whether you brush up your skills with a new language or want to plan a trip abroad. Now the Corona time is calling you to enhance your to-do not list. It is a time to add one more line to your hobby. You can learn it easily and come out of your depression and show your talent to others in your favorite language.

Self-esteem. This is the most effective part of my list of self-esteem. Raise your strength; raise your power to become better and healthier.

Self-esteem is not like another to-listed. It is recognizing your thoughts, love, feels, and presence. Put yourself in front of the mirror and say those words that make you feel proud and wonderful.

Dress up your style. Make yourself deaf and blind to what others think about you.

- Identify yourself.
- Understand yourself.

- Love yourself more.
- Then you will realize your importance.

Do not bend so much that others break you up easily. Rather get up so much that the other will stumble upon seeing you.

<u>Identity is to identity</u>. Take your time so you can learn new things and come out of your bubble. Everything that others say, not yours, it is time to prove them. Don't spare yourself in this Corona time to use it and learn it. There are lots of things that you can learn easily, provided you need discipline with yourself. Make your to-listed before bedtime and wake up with full of energy to fulfill it. There are a wider range of skills you just have to enroll yourself according to your interest.

Chapter -26: A Motivation Need to Boost in Your Life

"It's kind of overwhelming right now ... I can barely walk. I'm tired and sore, but really happy to have finished" – Chris Connelly.

Nothing in life is worthwhile, unless you take risks. There is no passion to be found playing small and settling for a life that's less than the one you can live. When you are deciding what you want to do in your life, people have told you to make sure you have something to fall back on, but we never understand that concept without having something to fall back on. If I will fall I don't fall back onto something or I don't want to fall forward. At least this way I figure out what I will hit. Without consistency you will never finish, so do what you feel passionate about.

Take chances, don't be afraid to be failed. There is an old IQ test in which there were 9 dots and you have to draw all the dots in line without lifting the pen. There was only possibility to draw that was by going outside the box. Don't be afraid to be creative. Don't be afraid to fall big. To dream big but remember dreams without goals is just dreaming. People remember the home runs, fall forwards. Thomas Edison conducted 1000 failed experiments because the 1001 was the light bulb.

Every failed experiment is one step closer to success. Take risks and I am sure you probably heard that before but understand why it is so important. You will fall in your life, accept it, you will lose, you will embarrass yourself, will suck at something. There is no doubt about it. There is an old saying you hang around the barber shop enough eventually you will get a haircut. So will catch a break but don't catch a break. The point is, everybody has a talent and a training to succeed, but do you have a gut to fall? If you don't fall, you are not even trying. To get something you never had, do something you never did.

Imagine you are on your deathbed and standing around your death bed is the ghost representing your unfulfilled potential, the ghost of the ideas you never acted on. The ghost of a talent you didn't use and they are standing around your bed, angry, disappointed and upset. They say we came to you because you could have brought us to life and now we have to go to the grave together. So, think today, how many of the ghosts will stand around the bed when the time comes?

There are many parts of the world who are suffering the poverty, malnutrition, starvation and so on. The world needs a lot and we need to fulfill. Go up there and give away whatever you have. Whether it's your time, your talent, your prayers, or your treasures. What you will do with what you have today. Sometimes, it's the best way to figure out where you are going your life will never be a straight path. Taking risks is not just about going for a job, it's also about knowing what you know and what you don't know. It's about being open to people and to ideas. The chances you take, the people you meet, the people you love, the faith that you have, that's what will define you. Never be discouraged. Never hold back. Give everything you got and when you fall throughout your life, remember this fall will bring happiness.

Chapter -27: How to Stop the Midyear Burnout from Someone

"The only thing that will make you happy is being happy with who you are, and not who people think you are" – *Goldie Hawn.*

Mitch Wallis whose age 27 years, used to be mountaineering the ranks at Microsoft, flying enterprise-class, assembly celebs and pitching snazzy new merchandise to Silicon Valley bigwigs. But under the floor of his apparently Instagram perfect life, there used to be turmoil.

'My ego cherished it, however, my physique sensed the affects', Sydney intellectual fitness suggests informed Huff Post Australia.

'For me, what that regarded like was once all my underlying intellectual fitness problems surfacing, being aggravated and all components of my existence deteriorating as a result of that'.

Wallis, who grew up in the north shore suburb of Mosman, has suffered from intellectual sickness from the age of eight. He used to be recognized with obsessive-compulsive sickness after his mum noticed him repetitively touching objects and blinking, however; he stated it got here to the floor when the strain of his company life styles pushed him to the brink in his mid-twenties.

'Not the sheer demand of work however additionally my personal expectation and the subculture of overall performance attempting to supply at a specific level,' he stated of his first journey with burnout. 'It took its toll'.

Living away from a household in the United States, Wallis was once so burnt out from work stress he grew to be incapacitated and ended up in an outpatient hospital in Louisville, Kentucky, for treatment. Looking again, his clearest reminiscence was once telling his mum over the phone. 'I don't suppose I can get better from this'.

Wallis got better and now dedicates his life's work to empowering younger human beings to share their intellectual fitness testimonies is clarity through heart on my sleeve.

We spoke to Wallis and different professionals about how to spot signs and symptoms of burnout and control it when it sneaks up.

What sincere is burnout?

Last year, it classified burnout with the aid of the World Health Organization (WHO) as an 'occupational phenomenon', legitimizing the experiences of many who've fallen prey to the problem, additionally regarded as imperative exhaustion.

'Burnout is a syndrome conceptualized as ensuing from continual administrative center stress that has now not been effectively managed,' stated WHO.

What are the signs and symptoms of burnout?

Burnout may also sense like decreased enthusiasm for work you formerly felt passionate about, Wallis explained.

'Despising work and seeing it as the enemy, bodily exhaustion or sickness, decreased overall performance and engagement are signs', he said, adding, 'It can additionally seem to be like a spike of common intellectual unwell fitness symptoms, like anxiety, agitation or depression'.

Burnout is one-of-a- kind for everyone, so it's vital to test in with how you're feeling and be aware of your emotions or behavior change. If you note a change, don't pass by it.

'For me, it begins with sleep disruption, irritability, and everyday anxiety', Wallis said. 'As it starts off grown to ramp, it receives greater acute the place my obsessional questioning will increase. My potential to deep sure eventualities or ideas from my head will become extra difficult. I'll experience depressed for no actual reason, and I get depersonalization, the place I experience barely dissociated and numb to a factor of it totally intruding on my life'.

<u>Strategies to forestall it.</u> 'We stay in an age of this unrealistic expectation and understanding of the rise-and-grind younger working professional,' Wallis said.

'Not the whole thing has to be accomplished today. We don't want to self-actualize this week. Become a ruthless prioritize and be aware of what 20% of matters will provide you 80% of the outputs I need'.

'Ask yourself what is the motive for this relentless pursuit or tempo that you are inclined to sacrifice your very own fitness or happiness for? And also, 'Who are you doing this for?' Wallis said.

'Your obligation is to locate that line and have the recognition and self-discipline to understand when the unhelpful narratives and faith structures have to take control'.

While acknowledging that corporations strain personnel with job needs and inflexibility and that places of work have a long way to be responsible for their body of workers members' intellectual heat, it's up to the worker to parent out what's using them and set boundaries.

Build your identification backyard or work

'What are you doing outdoor of the backyard to get extra price and well worth on the inside?' Wallis asked. 'Hobbies, learning, relationships, being a precise human to your fellow humans. These depend on the most'.

Burnout is regularly shut when you dwell for the weekend and have an all-or-nothing way of thinking. 'When humans say, 'I hate Mondays', or 'Thank God it's Friday', these are adorable little saying, however, what you're telling yourself is, '80% of my lifestyles sucks', stated medical psychologist Ryan Howes.

Bringing your weekend into your week and discovering engagement some place else can be a section of this strategy.

'If your weekends are stuffed with connecting with pals and getting some relaxation and going on brief adventures, fantastic. How can you make that section of your workweek?' Howes said. Examples Howes provided are getting breakfast with a non-work pal or going to a bookshop on your lunch break.

<u>Don't do it alone.</u> 'There is a historical saying,' 'If you favor to go fast, go alone. If you favor to go far; go together,' Wallis said. 'Vulnerability is key. Being able to say, 'Hey, I want to assist on this' is so important'. Wallis brought that many humans' trust in this idea however doesn't take motion it.

I suggest nothing comes from a single person. Everything is a crew effort, and we want to learn on every different when we are worn out so we can be in it for the marathon, now not the sprint.

<u>Take self-care and don't compromise on it</u>.

'Self-care is each reactive and proactive', Wallis explained.

Reactive self-care is out to tools, human beings, and mindsets that assist us with electricity and stability. They are the matters that put us again in a headspace of 'I brought this I can cope'.

Proactive is our work stream to make certain there is an always-on strong basis that we can use to thrive and no longer keep away from pitfalls, from bloodies showers to work out and the lot in between, it's the matters we do not remember how we are feeling so we have buffer room or a financial savings reserve of strength to face into when we want it.

Even if we have these plans or habits, they are vain until we move them. Discipline and no longer compromising is the distinction between success and failure in heading off burnout.

The Next Big Thing in Premature Preparation for Success

Stephen has described the first habit of most effective people as Pro-activeness. Proactive means that you are prepared for future events. A poet had also made the same point that 'keep the ship before the storm comes'. Do something every day that you are doing not for today but for tomorrow. If you look at the surrounding people, you know that most of the people in our society are engaged in the work of today or the past, while these people are worried about the future. But they did it to fix it, nothing happens.

If you are proactive, then you are one of the most effective people in the world, and if you are not, then you have to think about it. Successful people are those who slight things besides today's work are of no use today but hope to see very beneficial results. If you are doing this, then you are a visionary person. A visionary person is one who has dreamed of his future, a future is in front of his eyes, and he has kept his goal in his eyes. So first you have to create Pro-activeness within yourself.

Education has the most to do with the future. It has to shape the future of the nation tomorrow, so it is very important for teachers to be proactive. You may have heard the prayer of Prophet (peace be upon him) that either God will open my heart and remove the stigma of my tongue and make my task easy for me so they may understand my words. This prayer contains the complete message for the teacher.

If this were to happen, then there would be no need for Moses. The teacher is needed when he has to make an ordinary child a masterpiece and then we have to learn the tasks by which we can train him and make him a masterpiece; We have to change the way we work is.

For example, if your child is playing and there is an obstacle, you will be anxious about it and your full attention will be on the child so that does not fall into the obstacle. Will stop before you go. In the same way, you should be concerned about your students. Monitor them because that's what will make your students masterpieces. If the children in the last row know that the teacher is watching them all the time, then understand that those children will also start listening to you with full attention. If the child knows this observation of the teacher, he will not make a mistake. The child meets the artist when he is convinced that the teacher does not know, and then he does everything in the class that is not allowed.

The biggest problem with teachers is that they continue to use the old methods, whereas in today's world there is a lot to do every day. Teachers should also use alternative teaching methods. Adapt your teaching style to the advanced age. Don't associate your performance with the salary that we get paid so much we can only read in it. Bring your work to the forefront and learn the skills that will make your students masterpieces. Always be aware of the latest inventions and innovations in your articles.

There is good and evil in every human being, anger and peace, hatred and love. Our elders used to say that a good person is one who removes unnecessary things from within. Now all you have to do is remove the things that stand in your way. An excellent teacher is the one who trains himself first, starving the wolf inside him. Things we don't care about to go out of our minds. Stop giving importance to the negative things of your personality and give importance to the positive ones, praise them and like to listen. It is said that it is praise that makes a small thief a talented thief, and it is praise that makes a small doer the best man in the world.

Always keep in mind that what we can do today, we will not do tomorrow, so we have to do it today. No one in the world can go back but everyone can go forward, so we have to think ahead and spend every new day as the first day of life, do new things with new creativity. The only thing in the past is to learn the mistakes and think about the future.

Keys to create astonishing levels of success and happiness in their lives through universal principles are as below:-

Commitment. *Commitment unlocks the doors of imagination, allows vision, and gives us the right stuff to turn our dream into reality –* **James Womack.**

An open mind (Receptiveness). *Do the thing and you will be given the power –* **Ralph Waldo Emerson.**

<u>Flexibility</u>. *Stay committed to your decisions, but stay flexible in your approach –* **Tony Robbins.**

<u>Faith</u>. *Faith is taking the first step even when you don't see the whole staircase –* **Martin Luther King, Jr.**

<u>Thankfulness (Gratitude)</u>. *When I started counting my blessings, my whole life turned around –* **Willie Nelson.**

<u>Passion</u>. *There is no passion to be found playing small – in settling for a life that is less than the one you are capable of living –* **Nelson Mandela.**

Could You Please Leave A Review on the Book?

One last time!

I'd love if you could leave a review about the book. Reviews may not matter to big-name authors; but it is a tremendous help for authors like me, who don't have much following. It help me to grow my readership by encouraging folks to take a chance on my books.

To put it straight – reviews are the life blood for any author.

Please leave your reviews in the book review page.

It will just take less than a minute of yours, but will tremendously help me to reach out to more people, so please leave your reviews happily.

Thank you for supporting my work and I'd love to see your review on the book for my happiness.

Copyright © 2020 by Joseph Neyyan

ABOUT THE BOOK

Who doesn't want to be happy? Everyone seeking the meaning of happiness in life, which is the inspiration to the title. What is the key to happiness in life? Today, we are leading our lives in mindless pursuit, unable even to articulate what we are pursuing. Unlock your mind to become happiness through methodical solutions has given in this book. The secret of happiness has been brought forth, which create happiness within you, your family and relationships around the world.

KEY TO HAPPINESS help you to be happier and more resilient to life's turmoil. The latest scientific studies are put forth to construct a set of evidence based on practical actionable procedure. It will help you to connect with people, nature your relationships and find solutions. You'll get ideas for taking care of your body, making the most of what's good, and finding alternative ways to focus your mind.

A **motivational** self-help book that will transform and force to rethink on life on what is critical importance. **Believe in yourself, develop your confidence, stop procrastinating, overthinking, frustration, minimize stress, gain emotional freedom** and **achieve your goals** for lasting happiness.

If you're under **stress** and **strain**, feeling **depressed** and **frustrated** in life then this book is the solution for you.

If you wish to bring more happiness and unadulterated joy into your life, then this book is for you.

Are you tired? Unmotivated? Unexcited? Then this book is definitely for you. So what are you waiting for? Grab your book of **Key To Happiness** today.

ABOUT AUTHOR

Exploring the world of books, researching writers, read author blogs, and more. Attended the `CMS Higher Secondary School' which is affiliated to Central Board of Secondary Education, New Delhi. After completing the formal part of his education, he graduated from the Indira Gandhi National Open University, New Delhi, Thereafter enrolled in the Army and served the nation for 28 long years and retired as a Junior Commissioned Officer.

Now enjoying the privilege of being able to write full time, he is committed to producing books on nonfiction (personal development) that not only inspire and challenge people but also inspire in living life that is more rewarding and fulfilling. He is also a blogger and You Tuber. If you enjoyed this book, make sure to check out on his forthcoming works.